ZIONSVILLE INDIANA PUBLIC LIBRARY

W9-AAW-944

Visit the Library's On-line Catalog at:
http://www.zionsville.lib.in.us

Call the Library for information on access
if internet is not available to you.
(317) 873-3149

On-line magazine index with full text at:
http://www.inspire-indiana.net

NATURAL DISASTERS

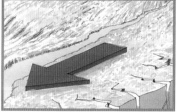

Artist:

Nick Hewetson was educated in Sussex
at Brighton Technical School, England, and studied
illustration at Eastbourne College of Art. He has
since illustrated a wide variety of children's books.

Consultant:

John Cooper is a geologist and Keeper of
the Booth Museum of Natural History in Brighton,
England. He has written several books on geological
topics, including dinosaurs and volcanoes and has
acted as consultant on many others.

Editor:

Karen Barker Smith

Author:

Jenny Vaughan lives in London,
England. She has written and edited children's
books on a variety of subjects. These include
several science titles and books on dinosaurs
and other prehistoric information books. Her
special interest is the environment and the
natural world.

Series creator:

David Salariya
was born in Dundee, Scotland,
where he studied illustration and
printmaking. He has illustrated
a wide range of books and has
created many new series of books
for publishers in the UK and
overseas. In 1989 he established
The Salariya Book Company.
He lives in Brighton with
his wife, the illustrator
Shirley Willis, and
their son.

© The Salariya Book Company Ltd
MCMXCIX

All rights reserved. No part of this book may
be reproduced, stored in a retrieval system or
transmitted in any form or by any means, electronic,
mechanical, photocopying, recording or otherwise,
without the written permission of the copyright
owner.

Created, designed, and produced by
**THE SALARIYA BOOK
COMPANY LTD**
25 Marlborough Place,
Brighton BN1 1UB

ISBN 0-531-14583-2 (Lib. Bdg.)
ISBN 0-531-15434-3 (Pbk.)

First American Edition 1999 by
Franklin Watts
Grolier Publishing Co., Inc.
Sherman Turnpike
Danbury, CT 06816

Visit Franklin Watts
on the Internet at:
http://publishing.grolier.com

A catalog record for this title is
available from the Library of
Congress.

Repro by Modern Age

Printed in Singapore.

NATURAL DISASTERS

Written by
JENNY VAUGHAN

Illustrated by
NICK HEWETSON

Created and designed by
DAVID SALARIYA

W
FRANKLIN WATTS
A Division of Grolier Publishing
NEW YORK • LONDON • HONG KONG • SYDNEY
DANBURY, CONNECTICUT

HUSSEY-MAYFIELD MEMORIA
Public Library
Zionsville, IN 46077

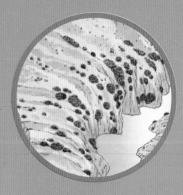
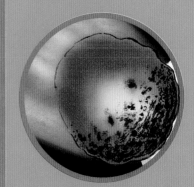

Contents

The atmosphere is the blanket of gas that surrounds the Earth. The mixture of gases — including nitrogen, oxygen, and carbon dioxide — gets thinner the farther it is from the surface of the Earth. The outermost layers are the exosphere and magnetosphere.

Exosphere

Magnetosphere

Thermosphere
Approximately 310 mi (500 km) thick.

Mesosphere
Approximately 22 mi (35 km) thick.

Stratosphere
Approximately 22 mi (35 km) thick.

The area of atmosphere above 50 mi (80 km) is also referred to as the ionosphere because the air is full of electrically charged particles called ions.

Troposphere
This is between 3.7 and 12 mi (6 and 18 km) thick and contains almost all the gas in the atmosphere, including water vapor (water in the form of gas). The troposphere is where weather occurs.

Hydrosphere
This is another name for the water that covers two-thirds of the Earth's surface, mainly in the oceans. Just as winds move air across the surface of the Earth, so currents flow through the waters of the oceans.

Crust
The Earth's crust is the tough, outer surface of the Earth. On average, it is about 19 mi (30 km) thick under land, but under mountains it can reach 43 mi (70 km). It is only about 4 mi (7 km) thick beneath the oceans.

Lithosphere and Asthenosphere
Beneath the crust lies the Earth's mantle. The outermost layer of the mantle is attached to the crust. The two together are called the lithosphere and are about 62 mi (100 km) thick. Below these is the next layer of the mantle, the asthenosphere.

Mantle
The mantle makes up about nine-tenths of the Earth. It extends 1,740 mi (2,800 km) down to the Earth's outer core. The asthenosphere is made up of hot, soft rock, over which the plates of the lithosphere move.

Outer Core
Beneath the mantle lies the Earth's outer core, which is about 1,398 mi (2,250 km) thick. No one has ever seen it, but scientists believe it is made up mainly of iron and nickel. Temperatures in the outer core are about 9932°F (5500°C). The metal here is molten (liquid).

Inner Core
The inner core is also metal and is about 758 mi (1,220 km) thick. Scientists believe its temperature is probably about 10,832°F (6,000°C). Metal at such a high temperature would normally be molten, but the huge amount of pressure from the other layers of the Earth causes it to be solid.

Where the edges
of the plates that make
up the Earth's crust meet,
they can push against each other so
hard that the crust is forced upward. This
action forms mountains called fold mountains.
The Himalayas are fold mountains, formed by the
landmass of India colliding with Asia.

The Earth

Natural disasters happen without any person causing them. They occur because of the way the Earth is made.

The Earth is surrounded by a blanket of gases, called the atmosphere. The gases close to the Earth make up the air we breathe. Air moves over the Earth's surface as wind, carrying warmth and rain, which we need for survival. But winds reaching high speeds become dangerous hurricanes, and the heavy rain they bring can cause floods.

The outermost layer of the Earth itself is called the crust. Beneath this is another layer, called the mantle. The crust and the top of the mantle are divided into huge sections called plates, which float and move on the lower mantle beneath. At the edges of some plates, the crust plunges down into the mantle or is forced upward. Some plates may slide past each other. An earthquake occurs whenever there is a violent movement of the crust. Volcanoes erupt at weak points in the crust, where molten rock called magma is forced up from beneath the Earth's surface.

The Earth is constantly changing. Over millions of years there have been enormous changes to the climate — it has gone through several long periods of immense cold. The plates that make up the Earth's crust move slowly but continuously, carrying the landmasses that make up the continents with them. Millions of years ago the Earth looked very different than it does today. In millions of years time it could be a very different place again.

Death of the Dinosaurs

Dinosaurs were reptiles, a little like the reptiles of today, such as lizards and turtles. This means that they were probably cold-blooded and needed the sun's heat to warm their bodies and give them energy. Dinosaurs lived on Earth for nearly 200 million years. There were many different types, from small, swift ones to heavy, lumbering plant-eaters and savage hunters. Suddenly, 65 million years ago, they disappeared — why?

One theory is that they were killed when an asteroid crashed into the Earth from space. This would have caused earthquakes and volcanic eruptions that would have thrown up so much dust and poison gas that the world was dark for months. There would have been a long, cold winter, which the cold-blooded dinosaurs could not survive. They would have died out, leaving only creatures such as the warm-blooded birds and mammals to survive.

A crater off the coast of Mexico (see map, below) shows that an asteroid (small planet) or meteorite (rock) landed there from space about 65 million years ago. It was so big it would have caused an explosion as powerful as 10,000 nuclear bombs, destroying everything up to 310 mi (500 km) away.

As the asteroid burned, the thick cloud of poisonous gas and dust it made could have caused a change in the climate. However, some scientists think the climate was getting colder anyway, so the asteroid and volcanic eruptions just made this happen faster.

Meteor Crater, in Arizona, was formed some time in the last 50,000 years when a meteorite hit the Earth. The crater is 3,937 ft (1,200 m) wide.

Ammonite (sea-creature) fossil

All of what we know about dinosaurs comes from their fossils, or remains found in ancient rocks. Scientists can figure out the age of the rocks where the fossils are found. From this, they can tell when the fossilized creature died. No dinosaur fossils have been found in rocks less than 65 million years old, so we know they must have died out then.

Dinosaur fossils

Many scientists believe dinosaurs died out when the world's temperature dropped, because they needed warmth to stay alive. Also, as the climate grew colder, there may not have been enough for them to eat. Warm-blooded mammals, birds, and smaller reptiles survived, but the dinosaurs, pterosaurs (flying reptiles), and plesiosaurs (swimming reptiles) became extinct.

Pompeii
The Eruption of Vesuvius

At about midday on August 24, in A.D. 79, the Roman city of Pompeii was destroyed by one of the most famous volcanic eruptions ever. Pompeii was a busy port on the coast of Italy, and nearby were two other towns, Stabiae and Herculaneum. All three were close to Mount Vesuvius, a volcano that was believed to be extinct (would never erupt again). No one in the surrounding towns was prepared for Vesuvius's eruption.

Although this disaster happened nearly 2,000 years ago, we know a lot about it because a man called Pliny the Younger, aged 17, wrote an eyewitness account. A "black and dreadful" cloud, full of flames, made the area "as dark as a sealed room without lights." Small stones started to fall from the sky like hail. Some people tried to run away, while others shut themselves in their houses. Then a cloud of burning gas and ash swept down the mountain. Pliny reported that it spread out "like a flood," burning and suffocating everyone in its path. At Herculaneum, it killed thousands more on the beach as they tried to escape.

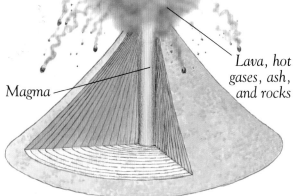

Magma

Lava, hot gases, ash, and rocks

How a Volcano Works

Volcanoes form mostly at the edges of the plates that make up the Earth's crust. Pressure from the mantle beneath forces molten rock, called magma, toward the Earth's surface, forming a volcano. When magma reaches the Earth's surface, it is called lava. As the volcano erupts, lava, hot gases, and ash pour out of its crater. Some eruptions are violent explosions, while in others, lava pours down the side of the volcano, hardening into rock as it cools.

During the first part of the eruption, Vesuvius sent out a deadly rain of ash and small pieces of solidified lava. This quickly piled up in the streets. People who had stayed indoors were soon trapped. Those who made it outside had to struggle over the deep layer of ash and stones or be buried in it. When the cloud of burning gas flowed down the mountain, it killed everyone, both indoors and out.

Before the eruption, magma and gases built up inside Vesuvius. They burst from the volcano in a violent explosion.

The lethal cloud of gases and hot ash began to fall to Earth. The wind helped blow it in the direction of the nearby towns.

Burning gas, ash, and molten rock, heated to about 887°F (475°C), then flowed down the mountain at high speed.

After the Eruption

All three towns of Pompeii, Herculaneum, and Stabiae were completely buried in ash and rocks. About 16,000 people died in Pompeii. The eruption blew away the whole center of Mount Vesuvius. Pompeii and the other towns were almost forgotten until, in the mid-1700s, Herculaneum and Pompeii began to be excavated.

Today, visitors can see Pompeii's ruined buildings and walk along the ancient streets. The pictures painted on the walls and even graffiti written long ago can now be seen. Visitors can imagine being in Pompeii the day it was destroyed.

In the 1860s, an archaeologist named Guiseppe Fiorelli found a way of making life-size models of people whose bodies were buried in ash in Pompeii.

The bodies of people buried in the eruption had rotted away, leaving a hollow space in the hardened ash. Fiorelli poured plaster of Paris into this space.

When the plaster became solid, Fiorelli chipped away at the ash. This would uncover the plaster cast of someone who had died on August 24, in A.D. 79.

Earthquakes

The city of San Francisco, in California, lies close to a crack in the Earth's crust called the San Andreas fault. Faults are often found at the edges of the plates that make up the crust. The rocks along a fault may become jammed against each other and not move for many years. But eventually, pressure builds up and the rocks suddenly break apart. The edges of the fault move violently, causing an earthquake.

Today there are strict rules to make sure buildings in San Francisco are as safe as possible in an earthquake. But these rules did not exist in 1906, when the worst earthquake ever to hit the United States happened there.

The earthquake of 1906 had its epicenter (center at ground level) in the San Francisco area. Tremors (shaking) may spread for hundreds of miles.

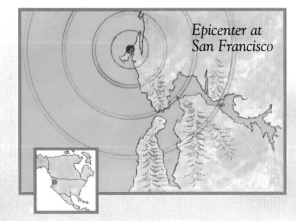

Epicenter at San Francisco

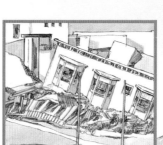

If vibrations from an earthquake are moving through loose soil, sand, or soft rock, the shaking ground starts to behave almost like a liquid. Buildings on ground that has "liquefied" in this way fall over or sink (left).

Epicenter

Focus

Stresses in the Earth's crust force rocks deep underground to break up and move. The place where this starts is called the focus of the earthquake. The epicenter is on the surface of the Earth directly above the focus. Earthquake damage is usually worst near the epicenter.

An earthquake in mountains can trigger a landslide or an avalanche (right) that will bury everything below it. An avalanche caused by an earthquake in Peru, in 1970, killed almost everyone in a town of 20,000 people. Only 92 survived.

Collapsing buildings are not the only dangerous result of an earthquake. Fires spread among damaged buildings (left), especially if gas and oil pipes are broken. Water supplies may be disrupted, and the many homeless people will need shelter and food. It is important to get rescue teams to an area struck by an earthquake as quickly as possible.

In 1988, an earthquake in Armenia destroyed the town of Spitak (above). As many as 100,000 people in Spitak and nearby towns may have died and more than 500,000 people lost their homes. The reason so many people died was because the buildings they lived in were not designed to stand up to earthquakes.

San Francisco Earthquake

Disaster struck San Francisco early in the morning on April 18, 1906. The roads began to move up and down like waves, and houses began to bend and sway. People were actually thrown out of their beds. Buildings came tumbling down. Many were made of wood and they were soon on fire. The main water pipes were damaged and firefighters could not put out the flames. They tried blowing up buildings to stop the fires from spreading, but this made things worse. Thousands of people were left homeless and had to leave the city or camp out in the open. More than 500 were killed.

An earthquake in Kobe, Japan, killed over 6,000 people in 1995 (above). Most new buildings in Japan are made to stand up to earthquakes, but in Kobe there were many older buildings, which were easily damaged and destroyed.

About 9,000 people died in an earthquake in Mexico City in 1985 (above). The epicenter of the earthquake was 250 mi (400 km) away, but because of the way the rocks and soil reacted under the ground, violent shocks were felt in the city.

Hurricanes and Cyclones

Hurricanes are violent storms that form over the warm seas of the Caribbean. They start out as thunderstorms. Warm, wet air close to the sea rushes upward, forming heavy clouds. These storms may band together, creating fast-moving winds that circle around a still center, or "eye." A typical hurricane can be about 373 mi (600 km) across. The scientific name for one of these storms is a tropical cyclone because they are common in the tropics — the area around the equator. The name hurricane is used for these storms when they occur in America. In the western Pacific, they are called typhoons, while in the Indian Ocean, they are cyclones.

Water vapor (water in the form of gas) in the rising air condenses to form thick clouds.

Torrential rain falls beneath.

Upward spiral of wind.

The eye of the storm.

Inside a Tropical Cyclone

A tropical cyclone forms as warm, damp air rises from near the surface of the sea. Winds of cool air blow in beneath it. The spinning motion of the Earth makes these winds travel upward in a spiral reaching around 30 mi (50 km) per hour, with gusts of 224 mi (360 km) per hour. In the middle of this swirling mass there is a calmer column of warm air, moving upwards and cooling at the same time. This is the eye of the storm.

Living with Storms

Living through a tropical cyclone can be terrifying. Wind flattens buildings and trees. Waves more than 26 ft (8 m) high crash in from the sea, and torrents of rain cause floods and landslides. In rich countries, people can be prepared for a tropical cyclone. They have strong homes and can make them even stronger by nailing boards over windows and doors. If things become really dangerous, good transport and organization helps people get away from the storm. But in poorer countries, things are more difficult. There are usually less materials and equipment available for preparing for the storms and for building shelters, and little money for rescue services.

Bangladesh is a poor country where most of the population are farmers. People must live where their crops grow, even if the area is in danger from floods and storms. They cannot escape easily, as roads are bad and transport is difficult. Their flimsy homes are quickly damaged, and if crops are spoiled, there may be nothing else to eat. In 1970, a cyclone struck (above) and killed up to 500,000 people.

Map showing direction that cyclones hit Bangladesh.

In 1991, a hurricane hit the coast of Florida. Huge waves crashed into southern Miami and caused an enormous amount of damage.

Plagues

The word "plague" usually refers to the deadly disease that is spread by the fleas that live on rats. It is also called the Black Death. In the mid-1300s, it killed approximately 30 million people in Europe and many more in Asia and Africa. Half the people in England died — there were so many bodies that people had to be buried in pits instead of proper graves.

There were two kinds of plague. The most common was bubonic plague. It caused a fever and dark swellings in a person's armpits and groin. Those affected usually died within a few days. Pneumonic plague affected the lungs, and it killed a person within hours. The Black Death in the 14th century was the worst outbreak of plague ever known. Today, the plague is only found in the poorest parts of the world.

Locust

Colorado beetle

Mosquito

Diseases that attack crops can do almost as much harm as ones that directly kill people. In the 1840s, potato blight, a disease caused by a fungus, killed potato crops in Europe (above). In Ireland, people depended heavily on potatoes for food. Without them, about a million people died of starvation or became so weak they died of other diseases. It became known as the Irish Potato Famine. A million more people left Ireland and never returned.

The Bible tells the story of how Moses led the people of Israel from slavery in Egypt. Before they left, ten plagues took place. Some were plagues of pests, others were diseases. One of the plagues was of frogs and toads. When the frogs died, there followed a plague of lice and a plague of flies. Scientists and historians believe the lice and flies arrived to feed on the bodies of the dead frogs.

Cool air billows out from the top of the storm and forms a huge circle of clouds.

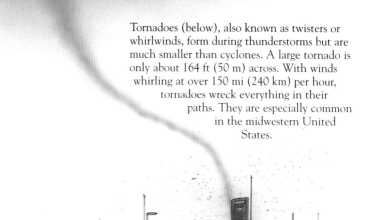

Tornadoes (below), also known as twisters or whirlwinds, form during thunderstorms but are much smaller than cyclones. A large tornado is only about 164 ft (50 m) across. With winds whirling at over 150 mi (240 km) per hour, tornadoes wreck everything in their paths. They are especially common in the midwestern United States.

In 1900 a hurricane hit the town of Galveston, Texas (above). A huge wave crashed in from the sea, killing at least 8,000 people. Often, the worst damage in a storm is done by waves like this. In Galveston, there is now a high seawall to protect the town.

Epidemics

When a disease spreads among a large number of people, it is called an epidemic. Different diseases spread in different ways. Many are caused by microorganisms (tiny living things). There are two main types of these — viruses and bacteria. Some bacteria are spread when creatures such as lice or fleas bite one person and then go to another. Bubonic plague is an example of this. Other bacteria are spread through water or air, or even by contact between people. Many diseases caused by bacteria can be cured using drugs called antibiotics. A scientist named Alexander Fleming discovered the first antibiotic, penicillin, in 1928.

Some diseases are caused by smaller organisms called viruses. Influenza (flu), for example, is caused by a virus. It is spread by people sneezing, coughing, breathing, and touching each other.

Sometimes the word plague is used to refer to a large number of pests. In Africa and Asia, plagues of locusts occasionally swarm over farmland, eating all the crops. Plagues of rats eat stored grain and may carry disease. A plague of Colorado beetles can destroy whole fields of potato plants, while mosquitoes spread the disease malaria.

Robert Koch (pictured above) was the scientist who discovered that the bacterium that causes cholera comes from human bodily waste. Cholera spreads when people drink water polluted with this waste. Koch also studied diseases such as tuberculosis (TB), bubonic plague, and malaria.

Around 1800, Dr. Edward Jenner discovered that people were immune to the disease smallpox if they had already had another, less dangerous disease called cowpox. Jenner had the idea of injecting people with cowpox so they became safe from smallpox. He called this procedure a vaccination. Worldwide vaccination has caused smallpox to disappear completely.

In the 16th century, Spanish invaders infected Aztecs with smallpox. Sketches from that period (right) show the suffering the disease caused.

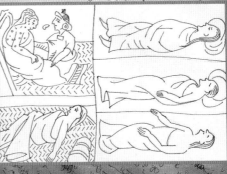

AIDS (acquired immune deficiency syndrome) is a killer disease caused by a virus. It can be passed on through sex with an infected person or through infected blood.

In 1918, just after the First World War, there was an epidemic of Spanish flu. More than 40 million people died from it all over the world.

"Mad cow disease"' comes from some types of cattle food. It damages cows' brains and kills them. People who eat meat from these cows are in danger of getting the disease themselves.

Fear of Floods

Rivers provide fresh water, which every living thing needs to stay alive. A river can be used by families, farmers, industries, and as a valuable transport route for boats to carry goods and people. It is for these reasons that villages, towns, and cities often develop near rivers.

Two mighty rivers flow through China: the Huang He and the Yangtze. Millions of people live close by them, working in factories and farming. One of the most important crops in China is rice, which grows in paddy fields — areas of land covered in ankle-deep water. But living and working near rivers can be dangerous. When water from melting snow pours into a river, or after heavy rains, there is a serious chance of flooding.

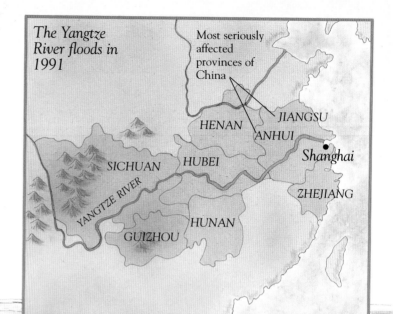

The Yangtze River floods in 1991

Most seriously affected provinces of China

HENAN

JIANGSU

ANHUI

SICHUAN

HUBEI

Shanghai

ZHEJIANG

YANGTZE RIVER

HUNAN

GUIZHOU

24

This map (left) shows how much of China was flooded in 1991. Floods in China are becoming more common, partly because too many trees near rivers have been cut down. Tree roots soak up rain and hold the soil together — without them, more water and mud pour into rivers.

In many parts of the world, people build large banks, called dikes, along rivers to try to contain the water (below). Dikes often need to be strengthened when there is a danger of serious floods, so that the force of so much water does not break through.

Snow melting in the mountains becomes wet and heavy. If there is a large amount, this snow can rush down the mountain as an avalanche, engulfing everything in its path. Avalanches in Austria in 1999 were some of the worst there on record. Nearly 40 people were killed at two ski resorts.

Earthquakes beneath the sea can cause huge tidal waves, or tsunamis (below). Out at sea, these are low, very broad waves. But close to the shore, they can rise to over 98 ft (30 m) high and travel inland at 370 mi (600 km) per hour. In 1998, tidal waves hit the coast of New Guinea, in the Pacific Ocean, killing about 2,000 people.

Destroyed by Water

When the Yangtze River flooded in 1931, over three million people were killed. In 1954, floods on the Yangtze killed 30,000. The 1990s have seen six serious floods there, and they seem to be happening more often. The floods in 1998 were the worst since 1954. So many people live along the Yangtze that saving them was a huge problem. Millions of homes and factories were destroyed, farm animals drowned, and crops were ruined. Soldiers spent weeks helping build up dikes along the river and getting people to higher ground. In spite of this, about 5,000 people died.

Weather Forecasting

When dangerous weather is on its way, being prepared can save lives. Weather forecasting has been studied for hundreds of years. In the past, meteorologists (scientists who study weather) used simple thermometers to measure air temperature and barometers to measure air pressure. Information from these helped them predict the weather. But the predictions were often not very accurate, so heavy rain and violent storms could still take people by surprise.

Today, meteorologists use modern thermometers, barometers, and other instruments to predict weather changes more accurately. Their studies include the movement of clouds, speed and direction of wind, and the amount of rainfall. Measurements like these are taken at thousands of weather stations all over the world — from oil rigs at sea, ships, and weather buoys. Aircraft and helium-filled balloons carry instruments high into the atmosphere to take meteorological readings. Radar is used to see where and how much rain is falling. Satellites above the Earth beam back photographs of clouds and information about weather systems around the planet. All this data is collected at weather centers and used to make weather forecasts.

Weather balloon

Barometer

Weather buoys have been used since the 1970s. They drift over the oceans measuring temperature, wind speed, air pressure, and humidity. Their transmitters send information from their instruments to satellites, which then beam them back to weather centers on land. Computers use this information to help forecast the weather.

Weather buoy

At weather centers (below), computers analyze the information received from the many instruments used in the air, on land, at sea, and on satellites. However, computers alone cannot predict the weather — expert meteorologists also study the information in order to make good weather forecasts for several days ahead.

Air presses on us from all directions. A barometer (above) is used to measure how strong this pressure is. Damp air has less pressure than dry air, so low air pressure means there is rain nearby. Barometers like this have been used for hundreds of years and are still used by amateur weather forecasters today.

Balloons filled with helium gas (left) are sent over 12 mi (20 km) into the atmosphere, carrying instruments that measure air pressure, temperature, and humidity. Information is also collected by aircraft, such as this one pictured below, which has been adapted for research. In the United States, special aircraft fly into hurricanes to monitor what is happening.

The weather forecasts we see on television (left) are planned at weather centers. The forecasters try to make the information simple and clear, so that viewers can understand what is happening to the weather and prepare for it. This is especially important for people who work outdoors, such as farmers. Forecasts for a few days ahead are getting more and more accurate, but long-range forecasts, for months ahead, are still difficult to get right.

Two types of weather satellites orbit the Earth. Geostationary satellites always stay above the same point on the surface, photographing the changing cloud patterns below. Meteorologists figure out wind speeds and directions from these photographs and can use them to track hurricanes. Polar-orbiting satellites travel from pole to pole, collecting information about temperature throughout the atmosphere and photographing the entire surface of the Earth a section at a time.

Polar-orbiting satellite

Geostationary satellite

Tropical cyclone seen from space

Glossary

Antibiotic
A medicine that kills bacteria and so cures the diseases caused by them.

Asteroid
A large rock or very small planet that orbits the sun. Asteroids sometimes get so close to Earth that they are pulled toward it by gravity and crash to the surface.

Avalanche
A mass of snow and ice tumbling rapidly down a mountain.

Bacterium
Singular of bacteria; micro-organisms, some of which can cause disease.

Black Death
Another name for the plague, a dangerous and infectious disease.

Cholera
A dangerous disease caused by bacteria found in polluted water.

Continent
A large mass of land.

Crust
The outer layer of the Earth. There are two kinds: the continental crust under the continents and the oceanic crust under the oceans.

Cyclone
Wind blowing in a circular motion. Tropical cyclones are made up of speeding winds and produce heavy rain. In the Indian Ocean area, the word "cyclone" refers to a tropical cyclone.

Epicenter
The point on the Earth's surface at the center of an earthquake, directly above the focus.

Equator
The imaginary line around the middle of the Earth.

Exosphere
The outermost layer of the atmosphere.

Fatal
Something that causes or results in death.

Fault
A crack in the Earth's crust.

Fold mountains
The type of mountains that are formed when two of the plates making up the Earth's crust push so hard against each other that they are forced upward.

Humidity
A measure of how much moisture there is in the air. High humidity makes people feel hot and sweaty.

Lava
The name for magma when it reaches the Earth's surface.

Liquefaction
The effect an earthquake can have on soft rocks or soil — making them behave like liquid.

Magma
Molten rock beneath the Earth's crust.

Magnetosphere
The layer of the atmosphere just below the exosphere.

Mantle
The layer of the Earth between the crust and the outer core.

Mesosphere
The layer of the atmosphere below the magnetosphere.

Meteorite
A large rock that falls from space to the Earth's surface. Meteorites often burn up on their way through the Earth's atmosphere.

Plague
A disease carried by the fleas of black rats from Asia. The word can also be used to describe large numbers of pests.

Pressure
Continuous force against something. Air exerts pressure on the Earth and everything on it. Pressure between rocks under ground can force them to move, causing an earthquake. Pressure building up in a volcano can cause an explosion and eruption.

Stratosphere
The layer of the atmosphere above the troposphere.

Tidal wave
See tsunami.

Tornado
A whirling funnel of high-speed wind occurring on land, most often in the United States.

Troposphere
The layer of the atmosphere nearest the Earth's surface. It contains the air we breathe, and it is where weather takes place.

Tsunami
A huge wave caused by an earthquake under the ocean.

Typhoon
The name for a tropical cyclone in the western Pacific area and China.

Vaccination
A method of protecting people against a disease.

Volcano
A mountain in which material from deep below the Earth's surface escapes to the surface during an eruption.

Water vapor
Water in the form of gas. When cooled, water vapor turns back into water.

Disaster Facts

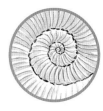

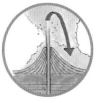

The "greenhouse effect" is caused by burning coal, oil, and similar fuels. This increases the amount of carbon dioxide in the atmosphere. Too much of this gas acts like a blanket, keeping the Earth warm and so changing the climate. If the climate gets warmer, the polar ice regions will melt and the sea will rise. Low-lying coastal areas and islands may be in danger of flooding or of even being completely covered by the sea.

The biggest natural disaster to hit life on Earth happened 250 million years ago. It was probably caused by volcanic activity filling the air with dust and chemicals that made the sea turn acid. Huge numbers of sea creatures were killed, as well as 90% of all four-legged land animals and many insects. Events like this are called mass extinctions. Another occurred 65 million years ago, when the dinosaurs died out.

Cyclone Tracy destroyed about 90% of the town of Darwin in Australia in 1974. Around 40,000 people lost their homes, but incredibly, only about 50 people were killed.

There were nearly 1,300 tornadoes in the American mid-west in 1992. Scientists study them using mobile research laboratories carrying radar to detect when tornadoes are forming. The most dangerous part of a tornado is when it touches the ground.

Tuberculosis (TB) is a lung infection that used to kill millions of people all over the world. In the mid-20th century, doctors were able to cure it with antibiotics. But now some types of tuberculosis bacteria have become resistant to such drugs. Tuberculosis is a special risk to people who have AIDS, as the virus makes it hard for their bodies to resist infections such as TB.

Malaria is one of the most deadly diseases on Earth. It is found mostly in tropical regions, such as Africa, where there are about 30 million cases a year. As the world's climate gets warmer, malaria may soon appear in non-tropical countries such as Britain.

When a volcano called Tambora erupted in Indonesia in 1815, it sent a cloud of ash into the air covering about 19 cubic miles (80 cubic kilometers). This was enough to change the weather around the world. The next summer was so cold and wet in Europe and North America that crops failed and many people went hungry.

In 1991, Mount Pinatubo, in the Philippines, erupted. It was the most violent eruption of the 20th century. About 200,000 people were moved out of the area, but in spite of this, over 1,000 people died.

The Richter scale is used to measure the amount of energy released in an earthquake. If an earthquake measures more than 6 on the Richter scale, there will be a lot of damage.

The Mercalli scale measures earthquakes according to how much damage they do. It ranges from I, which is hardly noticed, to XII, when almost everything is destroyed.

The most damaging earthquake in modern times happened in the city of Tangshan, in China, in 1976. It measured 8.3 on the Richter scale. 240,000 people were killed and 164,000 were badly wounded.

Hurricane Mitch struck Central America in November 1998 and killed more than 9,000 people. Most of these died in Honduras and Nicaragua. Homes, roads, and bridges were all destroyed and drinking water contaminated by the storm and the floods and

mudslides that followed it. Some scientists believe that landslides were made more likely because so much of the forests had been cut down — there were few trees to hold the soil in place during the heavy rainfall.

The Mississippi River flows from the north of the United States right down to the south. Dikes, called levees, have been built along the banks, but the river still overflows onto the low-lying floodplain around it. In 1993, Mississippi floods spread over nearly 31,000 sq mi (80,000 km^2). Thousands of people lost their homes, but because the United States has good warning and rescue systems, only 50 people died.

In 1953, floods caused by storms at sea swept 37 mi (60 km) inland in the Netherlands. Hundreds of people drowned. The same storm flooded many coastal areas in England and Belgium.

Drought can be just as disastrous as floods. When rivers and wells dry up, crops die and animals and people starve. There was an extremely severe drought in parts of Africa in the early 1980s. Year after year there was too little rain to grow enough food. Things were especially bad in Ethiopia in 1984-85. No one knows exactly how many died, but during the worst period more than 20,000 people were dying each month.

El Niño is a change in the way currents of warm water move in the Pacific Ocean. When this happens, weather over much of the world is affected.

The Huang He, or Yellow River in China is sometimes called China's Sorrow because it has caused so many deaths. In the last 3,500 years it has flooded almost every two years. In 1887, a huge flood broke through the dikes along its banks and flooded around 30,000 sq mi (78,000 km^2) of land. About 1.5 million people died.

Index

A
Africa 22-23, 31
AIDS 23, 31
air 6-7, 18-19, 23, 28, 31
air pressure 28-29
aircraft 28-29
antibiotics 23, 30, 31
Armenia 16
Asia 7, 22-23
asteroid 8, 30
atmosphere 6-7, 28-29, 31
Australia 31
Austria 26
avalanches 15, 26, 30

B
bacteria/bacterium 23, 30, 31
Bangladesh 21
Belgium 31
Black Death see plague
Britain 31

C
Caribbean 18
Central America 31
China 24-25, 31
climate 8-9, 31
clouds 18-19, 28-29
Colorado beetles 22, 23
crops 21, 22-23, 24, 27, 31
crust 6, 7, 10, 14, 30
cyclone see tropical cyclone

D
dikes 25, 27, 31
dinosaurs 8-9
disease 22-23, 31
drought 31

E
earthquakes 7, 8, 14-17, 27, 31
Egypt 22
El Niño 31
England 22, 31
epicenter 14, 17, 30
equator 18, 29, 30
eruptions 7, 8, 10, 12, 13, 31
Ethiopia 31
Europe 22, 31
extinct 9, 10, 31

F
fault 14, 30
Fiorelli, Guiseppe 13
fire 15, 17
fleas 22-23
Fleming, Alexander 23

floods 7, 21, 24-25, 27, 31
flu see influenza
focus (of earthquake) 14

G
gases 6-7, 8, 10, 12, 31
greenhouse effect 31

H
Honduras 31
humidity 28-29, 30
hurricane 7, 18-20, 21, 29, 31

I
Indian Ocean 18
Indonesia 31
influenza 23
inner core 6
ionosphere 6
Irish Potato Famine 22

J
Jenner, Edward 23

K
Kobe, Japan 17
Koch, Robert 23

L
landslide 15, 21, 31
lava 10, 30
levees see dikes
lice 22-23
liquefaction 14, 30
locusts 22-23

M
magma 7, 10, 12, 30
mantle 6-7, 30
mass extinction 31
Mercalli scale 31
Meteor Crater 8
meteorite 8, 30
meteorology 28-29
Mexico 8, 17
mosquitoes 22-23
mountains 7, 10, 12, 15, 26

N
Netherlands, the 31
New Guinea 27
Nicaragua 31

O
outer core 6

P
penicillin 23

Peru 15
Philippines 31
plague 22-23, 30
plates 7, 10, 14
Pompeii 10-13

R
radar 28, 31
rain 7, 12, 18, 21, 24, 28, 31
rats 22-23
rescue 15, 21
Richter scale 31
rivers
 Huang He 24, 31
 Mississippi 31
 Yangtze 24, 27

S
San Andreas Fault 14
San Francisco 14-17
satellites 28-29
seas 6, 18, 20-21, 27, 28, 31
snow 24, 26
Spanish flu see flu
starvation 22, 31
sun 8

T
temperature 6, 12, 28-29
thunderstorm 18, 20
tidal wave see tsunami
tornadoes 20, 30, 31
tropical cyclones 18, 20, 21
tsunami 27, 30
twister see tornado
typhoons 18, 30

U
United States 14, 17, 20-21,
 29, 31

V
vaccination 23, 30
Vesuvius 10-13
viruses 23, 31
volcanoes 7, 8, 10-13, 30, 31

W
water 6, 15, 17, 23, 24-27, 31
water vapor 6, 18, 30
weather 6, 28-29, 31
weather buoy 28
whirlwind see tornado
wind 6-7, 12, 18, 20-21, 28

HUSSEY-MAYFIELD MEMORIAL
Public Library
Zionsville, IN 46077